Original title:
Clouds and Sunshine

Author: Gabriel Kingsley
ISBN HARDBACK: 978-9916-88-910-7
ISBN PAPERBACK: 978-9916-88-911-4

Crafted Tales from Rays' Touch

In the morning light we find,
Stories woven, soft and kind.
Each beam a whisper, each glow a sign,
In the sun's embrace, our hearts entwine.

Shadows dance where moments play,
Casting dreams that drift away.
Nature's canvas, painted bright,
Crafting tales from rays of light.

Flickers of gold on fields of green,
In every corner, there's beauty seen.
Time stands still in this sacred space,
As memories linger, each one a trace.

The world awakens, silence breaks,
In the warmth, the spirit wakes.
Stories crafted in every hue,
From rays' touch, life feels anew.

Harmony of Brightness and Mist

In the dawn's soft embrace, light unfurls,
A tender kiss upon the curls.
Whispers of mist entwine in grace,
A dance of silence, a sacred space.

Golden rays through veils do weave,
In this moment, we believe.
Nature sings a tranquil song,
Where both light and shadow belong.

The Unexpected Union of Light and Shade

In the garden where shadows play,
Light and dark find their way.
A secret meeting in the grove,
Where beauty flourishes, dreams rove.

Through tangled branches, a glimmer flows,
A harmony of highs and lows.
Surprises bloom in every fold,
A tale of warmth in stories told.

Trails of Radiance in the Fog

Misty paths where secrets lie,
Glowing trails beneath the sky.
Each step whispers tales of light,
In the heart of the soft twilight.

Figures dance in the shifting haze,
Guided by the moon's gentle gaze.
Illuminated by nature's art,
A symphony that stirs the heart.

Soothing Caresses of Warmth and Mist

Embraced by warmth, the mist descends,
A gentle touch where time suspends.
With every breath, a sigh of peace,
In this bubble, worries cease.

Whispers of comfort in the air,
Λ tender moment, beyond compare.
Wrapped in a cloak of soft embrace,
The heart finds its perfect place.

Lullabies of Mist and Glow

Whispers weave through silken air,
Softly cradling dreams so rare.
Misty tendrils dance and flow,
In the night, the soft lights glow.

Gentle songs of twilight play,
Guiding stars till break of day.
Each note lingers, sweet and low,
Wrapped in warmth, the shadows grow.

Light Play between Shadowed Heights

Sunlight dapples through the leaves,
Beneath the arches, magic weaves.
Shadows stretch and softly sigh,
In this realm where eagles fly.

Glimmers whisper secrets old,
As the stories do unfold.
Between the peaks, the light does dance,
Inviting minds to take a chance.

Echoes of Dawn and Dusk

Morning breaks with golden rays,
Chasing off the night's deep haze.
Echoes linger, calm and bright,
As day surrenders to the night.

Fading hues of red and blue,
Blend together, fresh and new.
In this symphony of time,
Melodies of dusk and chime.

A Tapestry of Grays and Glimmers

Clouds envelop the fading sun,
Casting shadows, yet we run.
In the stillness, colors blend,
Grays and glimmers, paths extend.

Whispers of a world awash,
In the twilight, shadows thrash.
Each thread woven, storm or calm,
A tapestry, a soothing balm.

Celestial Contrasts

In the sky where shadows play,
Stars ignite the dusky gray.
Moonlit beams, a gentle guide,
Whispers of a world inside.

Clouds and colors intertwine,
Shifting hues, a grand design.
Day and night in soft embrace,
A dance of light, a timeless space.

Flickers Through the Mist

In the dawn, the fog does creep,
Softly waking from its sleep.
Light breaks through in gentle waves,
Revealing paths the silence saves.

Shadows dart and flicker bright,
Nature's breath, a pure delight.
Magic forms in every gleam,
Reality or just a dream?

Serene Silhouettes Above

Mountains crowned with twilight grace,
Stand as guardians, time won't erase.
Silent pines, their needles sway,
Guiding spirits in their play.

Stars emerge in velvet sky,
Eclipsing thoughts that linger high.
Stillness holds its breath so tight,
Cradling dreams in tranquil night.

The Brightness Beneath Whispering Veils

Beneath the shrouds of evening's hue,
Glow of secrets waits for you.
Veils of time, they softly part,
Revealing wonders of the heart.

Every whisper, every tone,
Tells of journeys yet unknown.
In the silence, truth prevails,
Bathed in glow where hope unveils.

Horizon's Embrace

The sun dips low, kissed by the sea,
Painting skies in hues of gold.
Whispers of twilight, soft and free,
In the hush, the stories unfold.

Breezes carry scents of night,
As shadows blend with glowing flame.
Stars emerge with silent light,
Each one calls out a secret name.

Flickering Hues, Fleeting Moments of Light and Cover

Fireflies dance in twilight's spell,
Chasing whispers through the air.
Moments captured, none can tell,
Of the magic hidden there.

Veils of dusk, so soft and light,
Wrap the world in gentle grace.
Fleeting echoes of the night,
In the dark, we find our place.

Glistening Drops and Warm Embrace

Raindrops glisten on the leaves,
Nature's jewels, pure and bright.
Each one holds a tale that weaves,
A symphony of deep delight.

Warmth of love in every glance,
Binding hearts in softest ties.
In the rain, we find our dance,
Underneath these endless skies.

Drifting Realms of Diffused Light

Mist hangs low, ethereal breeze,
Softly veiling the world anew.
In these realms, the soul finds ease,
As shadows blend with morning dew.

Floating dreams on silver tides,
Guided by the dawn's embrace.
In this dance where silence glides,
We discover our sacred space.

A Symphony of Rays and Tints

In the morning glow, colors blend,
Nature's canvas, hues ascend.
Each stroke a note, a vibrant sound,
In sunlight's warmth, joy is found.

Waves of red and gentle gold,
Stories of light, vividly told.
Every shadow dances near,
Whispers of beauty, crystal clear.

As daylight wanes, a soft embrace,
A masterpiece in time and space.
The palette shifts, the day concedes,
To twilight's grace, where magic breeds.

In the evening's calm, all is right,
The symphony ends with the night.
Yet in our hearts, the music stays,
A lasting tune, in endless rays.

Twilight's Gentle Brush

In the hush of dusk, colors blend,
Softening edges, as day does end.
A gentle sigh, the world transforms,
Wrapped in twilight, as silence warms.

Brush of lavender, deepening skies,
Crimson whispers, the daylight dies.
Stars peek out, one by one,
Painting dreams, now begun.

The moon emerges, a silver thread,
Guiding thoughts in our heads.
The horizon blurs, the night will call,
Under twilight's spell, we surrender all.

In this moment, time stands still,
With hearts alight, we feel the thrill.
As shadows play, in soft array,
Twilight speaks, in its own way.

Dunes of Light and Shade

In the desert's breath, shadows shift,
Golden grains that softly lift.
Sunrise glints on dunes so wide,
Where light and shade do dance with pride.

Waves of sand, like ocean tides,
In silent beauty, the landscape hides.
Footsteps whisper, stories untold,
In the embrace of warm, dry gold.

As the sun dips low, colors swell,
Crafting dreams where silence dwells.
Each ridge casts shadows, deep and long,
Nature's chorus, a haunting song.

In the night, when stars arise,
The softest light fills endless skies.
Dunes of dreams where spirits roam,
In the heart of night, we find our home.

Aurora's Silent Caress

In frozen nights, a dance begins,
With colors bright, the sky it spins.
Emerald greens and violet hues,
The aurora whispers, ancient truths.

Gentle waves in the winter night,
Glowing softly, a beautiful sight.
Nature's brush, in silent grace,
We feel her touch in cold embrace.

The world below, in stillness waits,
To witness wonders, as fate creates.
Streaks of light in endless flow,
Reveal the secrets the night will show.

In awe we stand, hearts open wide,
Cradled by beauty that won't abide.
Aurora sings, its serenade,
In silent caress, memories made.

A Dance of Spheres

In twilight's soft embrace, they spin,
Around the sun's warm gaze within.
Each twirl a note in cosmic song,
A harmony that feels so strong.

Gravity's pull, a sweet refrain,
As stars ignite, the dark turns plain.
Galaxies weave in a grand ballet,
Unfolding night to greet the day.

Radiant Whispers

Through crisp air, secrets softly roam,
In every breeze, they weave a home.
A murmur of dreams on velvet wings,
The world awakes, and softly sings.

Underneath the golden light,
Voices dance in sheer delight.
Whispers of hope in each soft breeze,
Caressing hearts like gentle trees.

Ephemeral Grace beneath an Aegis

Time drapes its veil, light as a sigh,
Moments capture the fleeting high.
Grace in each glance, a spark ignites,
In shadows cast by waning lights.

Beneath the arch of night's embrace,
Fleeting beauty finds a place.
Held tenderly in time's soft hands,
As silence weaves through golden sands.

Kisses of Brilliance on the Edge

At dawn where earth embraces dawn,
A million shades in blush are drawn.
Kisses of light where shadows play,
The edge of night gives way to day.

Each ray a promise, bright and bold,
Stories in colors yet untold.
Across the horizon's waking face,
A canvas bright, a warm embrace.

The Play of Dappled Light's Caress

Through leaves above, the sun weaves gold,
A tapestry of stories told.
Dappled light finds its gentle way,
In moments caught where children play.

Each flicker, a dance upon the ground,
Nature's laughter in joy unbound.
With every breeze, the world awakes,
A symphony of life that quakes.

Shades of the Tempest

Dark clouds gather in the sky,
Whispers of thunder, a distant sigh.
Winds of fury begin to moan,
Nature's power made widely known.

Lightning dances, bright and fierce,
In the heart of the storm, we pierce.
Rain falls heavy, a soothing song,
In the chaos, we all belong.

Colors clash with a vibrant roar,
Each drop a tale of ancient lore.
Yet in the tumult, a calm will rise,
To paint the world with clearer skies.

Harmony in the Heavens

Stars ignite in the velvet night,
Whispers of dreams take their flight.
Galaxies swirl in a timeless dance,
Inviting the heart to take a chance.

Moonlight bathes the earth in grace,
Softening shadows in this vast space.
Celestial music cools the air,
Binding all souls in a gentle prayer.

Each twinkling star, a story vast,
Echoes of futures and of the past.
In this symphony, we find our way,
Dancing in light where night meets day.

Dappled Horizons

Sunrise spills gold over the hills,
A canvas painted with tranquil thrills.
Trees stand tall, their branches sway,
As light breaks forth to greet the day.

Streams reflect the morning glow,
Nature's wonders begin to flow.
Fields adorned in colors bright,
Each petal whispers pure delight.

Clouds drift softly, a gentle sight,
Casting shadows in warm sunlight.
Horizons stretch with promise new,
Dappled beauty in every view.

Mirth in the Murk

In the shadows, laughter echoes,
Soft and warm like the evening meadows.
Hidden smiles and secret glows,
In the murky depth, joy still flows.

Through thickets dark, a path we tread,
Where silence speaks and hope is fed.
Life's gentle jest, a sweet surprise,
In the gloom, the spirit flies.

With every heartbeat, a flicker bright,
Illuminates the depths of night.
Mirth within the murk prevails,
A tale of courage that never fails.

Serenade of Silver Linings

In twilight's embrace, whispers sing,
Silver threads weave, a delicate string.
Stars ignite the night with their glow,
Hope dances lightly, as dreams start to flow.

Through shadows cast, a shimmer is found,
Soft melodies rise, so gentle, profound.
The heart gathers strength from the light,
Echoes of love turn darkness to bright.

In every sigh, a promise takes flight,
A serenade born from the canvas of night.
Embrace every glimmer, hold it so near,
For even in silence, sweet music we hear.

Hues of Radiance and Gloom

Brush strokes of fire contrast with the gray,
Radiance flickers, then fades away.
Each moment captured in vibrant frames,
Gloom drapes itself in sorrowful claims.

Yet within the dark, a color will blend,
Shadows recede, as the light will transcend.
In the depths of despair, hope finds its way,
Hues of resilience paint life's grand ballet.

With every sunset, a promise is spun,
Tomorrow awaits, the battle not done.
For even in darkness, beauty will bloom,
Radiant dreams reborn, dispelling the gloom.

Dancing Veils in the Sky

Clouds twist and turn, a dance in the air,
Veils of mist brush softly, with elegance rare.
Each gust of wind tells a story anew,
Colors of sunset, a celestial hue.

Stars join the dance, twinkling so bright,
Guiding the wanderers lost in the night.
In the silence above, laughter takes flight,
Echoing dreams in the moon's gentle light.

As dawn breaks the spell, the veils start to fade,
A new day's embrace, where night's magic laid.
Yet memories linger, a soft serenade,
Of dancing veils cradled in twilight's cascade.

A Canvas of Dreams and Brightness

Strokes of imagination paint wide and free,
A canvas alive with vibrant decree.
Each color tells tales, both bold and divine,
In the realm of dreams, all hearts intertwine.

Bright yellows of laughter, deep blues of the sea,
Greens of fresh hope, in harmony be.
Brushes of time sketch a future untold,
As whispers of art warm every soul bold.

In shadows of doubt, a masterpiece waits,
Inspiring belief as the mind resonates.
With passion and vision, let your spirit soar,
A canvas of dreams awaits to explore.

Echoes in Brightness and Murk

In shadows deep where secrets lie,
The whispers weave, a ghostly sigh.
Bright echoes dance on dusky streams,
Bringing forth forgotten dreams.

A flicker glints in twilight's gaze,
Illuminating the tangled maze.
In murk and light, they intertwine,
A tapestry of fate divine.

Each shimmer speaks of stories old,
In silent bursts, the truth unfolds.
From brightness born, in darkness found,
Life's echoes swirl all around.

The blend of light, the kiss of night,
Crafting visions, pure delight.
In every hue and gentle spark,
Life's whispers glow within the dark.

The Dreamlike Dance of Fluids and Lumens

In liquid realms where colors flow,
The lumens gleam, an endless show.
They swirl and twist, a rhythmic trance,
Inviting all to join the dance.

The water bends in silver hues,
Reflecting dreams and midnight views.
From rippling waves, a soft embrace,
A haunting grace, a stunning place.

Each droplet holds a sacred song,
In fluid realms, where we belong.
The pulse of light, the breath of sea,
Whispers secrets, wild and free.

The night unfolds with every tide,
Where lumens dwell, and dreams abide.
In this surreal and vibrant sway,
We lose ourselves and drift away.

The Interplay of Gloom and Glimmer

In shadows cast by the setting sun,
The gloom and glimmer, forever run.
They waltz upon the edge of night,
A delicate dance, dark and light.

Through thickets dense and moonlit fields,
The promise of dawn, the night's yields.
Each whisper bright, a haunting thrill,
In twilight tales, fate's quill.

A battle fought in silence deep,
The sorrowed sighs, the secrets we keep.
Yet glimmers spark, a fleeting chance,
To find our joy in this dark dance.

In ebb and flow, both sad and sweet,
Life's tapestry weaves all to meet.
In every crease, the shadows play,
A glimmer's glow will light the way.

Fading Whispers and Radiant Tunes

As fading whispers grace the air,
The echoes linger everywhere.
A symphony of soft farewell,
In every note, a tale to tell.

Radiant tunes burst forth with flair,
Their vibrant echoes fill the square.
With every strum and gentle beat,
The heart finds rhythm, bittersweet.

In twilight's breath, the silence stirs,
With fading light, the magic purrs.
Each whispered word sings through the night,
A lullaby of love and light.

As shadows blend with dawn's embrace,
The whispers fade, yet still, we chase.
In radiant songs that intertwine,
Life's fleeting moments, so divine.

Tints of Joy and Somberness

In the meadow where flowers bloom,
Joy dances like sunlight's loom.
Yet shadows whisper soft and low,
A contrast rich, a tale to show.

Laughter twirls on breezy air,
While silent sighs lurk everywhere.
Colors clash in life's great scheme,
A tapestry of joy and dream.

Through vibrant hues, we find our way,
In every smile and tear's display.
Joy and somberness blend and weave,
A story told for those who cleave.

In twilight's hush, they softly blend,
A dance of light that shall not end.
In every heart, a canvas wide,
With tints of joy and shadows tried.

Flutters of Light among Shadows Deep

In the forest where secrets lay,
Light flutters bright, chasing shadows away.
Its gentle touch, a warm embrace,
In darkness too, we find our place.

Amidst the trees where whispers creep,
Hope ignites in shadows deep.
Each ray of sun, a guiding star,
Leading us to dreams afar.

Through the dusk, the light will creep,
Awakening souls from their sleep.
With every flutter, hearts align,
In radiant moments, we entwine.

So let us dance where dark meets light,
In the harmony of day and night.
For even shadows lend their grace,
In this world, we find our space.

Embracing the Shades of the Bright

In the dawn, the colors play,
Each hue whispers, come what may.
Embracing shades both bold and slight,
In this journey, we find our light.

Through golden rays and silvery beams,
We weave together our wildest dreams.
Every tone tells a story true,
In the tapestry woven anew.

With every shade, a heartbeat found,
Echoing life, a sweet sound.
Embracing all, we learn to grow,
In every bright shade, love will flow.

So hold these colors close and dear,
For in their presence, we have no fear.
In the shades of love, so warm and bright,
We find our strength and purest light.

The Secret Life of Luminous Hues

In the quiet, colors stir,
A secret world where shades confer.
Whispers of light in hidden rooms,
Where every hue, a heart consumes.

Emerald greens and sapphire blues,
Share their tales in gentle cues.
The vibrant hues, they dance and sway,
In the secret life of each new day.

They pulse with dreams, they shimmer bright,
A hidden world, a pure delight.
In silence, they unveil their plea,
For every heart to simply see.

So wander forth, let colors guide,
To realms where light and shadows bide.
In luminous hues, our spirits rise,
The secret life reveals the skies.

Hearts of Warmth

In the quiet glow of twilight's breath,
Hearts unite, casting away the death.
With every pulse, a promise is spun,
A tapestry woven, two spirits as one.

Embers flicker beneath the stars,
Whispers of love, healing old scars.
Hands entwined, they dance in the night,
Sparks of connection, souls taking flight.

Souls of Gray

In shades of twilight, stories unfold,
Of dreams forgotten, and tales left untold.
Lost in the silence, where shadows play,
Souls wander gently through the shades of gray.

Echoes of laughter, now faint whispers,
Haunting the moments, where time lingers.
Yet in the stillness, there lies a spark,
A flicker of hope, igniting the dark.

Cradles of Luster in Dusk's Arms

Dusk wraps the world in a gentle embrace,
Cradling the dreams, that night may trace.
Stars begin to sparkle, a soft lullaby,
A cradle of luster, beneath the sky.

Whispers of magic in the evening air,
Each moment cherished, each heart laid bare.
In dusk's arms, worries start to fade,
A sanctuary found, where memories are made.

Beneath the Shroud

Beneath the shroud of a silken night,
Secrets are hidden from dawn's first light.
The world slows its pulse, a tranquil spell,
In the depths of darkness, where shadows dwell.

Softly they linger, the dreams unspooled,
In velvet whispers, the heart is ruled.
A dance of echoes, entwined and free,
Beneath the shroud, the soul dares to be.

Glimmers Expose

Glimmers expose where the heart's truth lies,
In the silent spaces, beneath the skies.
Each star a beacon, guiding the way,
Illuminating paths for the lost to sway.

In the still of the night, fears start to wane,
Hope rises softly, like dew on the plain.
Moments of clarity in shadows dance,
With every glimmer, life finds its chance.

The Magic Between Light and Shade

In the magic between light and shade,
Dreams intertwine in a vibrant parade.
Colors collide in a spectacular blend,
A place where beginnings and endings suspend.

Life's gentle rhythm sways to its tune,
Under the watch of a silver moon.
In this embrace, every heart can sing,
The magic between, the joy that it brings.

Ethereal Embrace of Daylight

The sun spills gold upon the trees,
Awakening whispers in the breeze.
A dance of shadows, soft and slow,
Where dreams arise in morning's glow.

Light twirls softly through the air,
Drawing smiles from hearts laid bare.
In this embrace, we find our way,
As night surrenders to the day.

Birds take flight with joyous song,
In this haven where we belong.
The world awakens, fresh and bright,
Cradled in the arms of light.

Time drifts gently, moments blend,
Each heartbeat whispers, "do not end."
In this ethereal, warm embrace,
We find our peace, our sacred space.

Radiant Tides of the Sky

Clouds cascade like waves on high,
A canvas brushed with hues that sigh.
Soft pastels swirl, deep blues ignite,
As day surrenders to the night.

Stars emerge like distant dreams,
In a dance of radiant beams.
The moon bathes earth in silver's grace,
Her light a tender, soft embrace.

Wind carries tales through the night air,
Whispers of love, secrets to share.
Beneath this vast, celestial dome,
We find in starlight, our true home.

The universe, a timeless sea,
Where heart and soul can just be free.
The tides of sky, enchanting and bright,
Guide us through the endless night.

The Hidden Palette Above

In twilight's hush, colors collide,
A hidden palette, rich and wide.
Soft gradients of red and blue,
Blend secrets only stars knew.

Brush strokes of clouds drift and weave,
A masterpiece that we believe.
Each evening sky, an artist's play,
Transforming dusk into a ballet.

Golden hues seep into the dark,
Igniting dreams with a gentle spark.
The canvas stretches, endless and deep,
Where beauty resides, and silence speaks.

We gaze upward, hearts entwined,
In every hue, a story defined.
The hidden palette above our head,
Paints the journey where dreams are fed.

Echoes of Warmth and Chill

In the embrace of morning light,
Warmth awakens, dispelling night.
Yet whispers of cool air draw near,
A dance of seasons, crisp and clear.

Leaves flutter down with autumn grace,
Their colors bright, a fleeting trace.
The chill invites us to come close,
In fireside's glow, we seek the most.

Winter's breath holds a silent weight,
Yet hearts ignite, this warmth creates.
As snowflakes fall like dreams set free,
We find in cold, sweet harmony.

Through every season, time will tell,
The echoes of warmth, the chilly bell.
In nature's rhythm, life unfolds,
A story of warmth in chill retold.

Tides of Brilliant Whiteness

Waves of foam crash on the shore,
A dance of light forevermore.
Sea birds call, their shadows glide,
In whiteness, the dreams abide.

The sun paints gold on softest sand,
Nature's touch, a gentle hand.
Salt and breeze in whispered tones,
The ocean speaks, it knows our bones.

Moonlight glimmers on the sea,
A silver path, so wild and free.
Tides that ebb and flow with grace,
Whiteness holds a sacred space.

In the quiet, watch it sway,
Magic lingers, night and day.
Through the whispers, secrets chase,
Tides of brilliance find their place.

Sun-kissed Caresses of the Ether

Morning light breaks through the cloud,
Shining soft, cheerful and loud.
Winds that carry scents of bloom,
The air is filled with sweet perfume.

Golden rays on fields of green,
In this moment, we convene.
Nature's warm embrace surrounds,
In quiet joy, our hearts are found.

Laughter dances in the air,
Every heartbeat, free from care.
Sun-kissed whispers, secrets shared,
In the ether, love declared.

Time stands still, the world afire,
In creamy dusk, our dreams aspire.
Each caress like fleeting light,
Moments cherished, pure delight.

Shadows Cast by Fading Warmth

The sun dips low, shadows grow long,
Silent echoes of a song.
Softly wrapped in twilight's hue,
Night embraces, calm and true.

Whispers linger in the air,
Fading warmth, a gentle care.
Trees stand tall, their silhouettes,
In the dusk, our heartache rests.

Stars appear, one by one,
A silver dance has just begun.
In the quiet, sorrows cease,
Shadows cast, a sense of peace.

The world seems small, dreams unfurl,
In twilight's grasp, we gently twirl.
Embracing night, we find our way,
Fading warmth at end of day.

Transient Gleams among the Vapor

Mist rises soft, like whispered sighs,
Veiling secrets, truth belies.
Gleams that shimmer, fleeting light,
In the vapor, day meets night.

Dreams drift softly through the air,
Caught in glimpses, here and there.
Ephemeral thoughts on gentle breeze,
Moments captured, time to seize.

Among the clouds, a dance begins,
Like the laughter that we spin.
Transient gleams, the world transforms,
In the vapor, beauty forms.

Embrace the mystic, fleeting thrill,
In wonderment, hearts stand still.
For in the haze, we come alive,
In every gleam, our spirits thrive.

Dreamscapes where Shadows Share

In twilight's hush, the shadows blend,
Whispering tales where dreams ascend.
Underneath the silver moon,
Time drifts softly, a gentle tune.

Veiled figures dance on softest grass,
Woven secrets, moments pass.
Colors shimmer in a silent sway,
As night embraces the fading day.

Each dream a leaf on the twilight stream,
Floating softly on the gentle beam.
In the realms where whispers dwell,
A world unfolds where all is well.

Awake or sleep, who can declare,
In the dreamscapes where shadows share.
The fabric of night, rich and rare,
Binds us gently in its tender care.

Flickers Beneath a Charcoal Dome

Beneath the dome of charcoal skies,
Flickers dance where the silent lies.
Stars emerge like distant sighs,
Dreams awaken, no goodbyes.

With every spark, a whisper shines,
Stories told through shadowed lines.
Glimmers of hope in the vast night,
Lighting paths with pure delight.

As the world fades in twilight's hold,
Flickers guide the young and old.
In this realm where shadows roam,
Hearts ignite, calling them home.

In the depths of night's embrace,
Every flicker finds its place.
Beneath the dome of charcoal dreams,
Life flows softly in quiet streams.

Breath of Zephyrs and Glows

The zephyrs whisper through the trees,
Carrying secrets with tender breeze.
In the dusk where colors blend,
A canvas painted, hearts transcend.

Amidst the glows of fading light,
Dreamers gather, hearts ignite.
Every breath, a story spun,
In this dance, all is one.

The night unfolds with gentle grace,
Embracing all in its warm embrace.
Stars awaken to the tender call,
As shadows deepen, night enthralls.

In the symphony of the fading day,
Zephyrs sing in a blissful play.
Breathing life into the still night,
Guiding dreams in their gentle flight.

The Symphony of Softness and Glow

In the hush of night, a symphony plays,
Softness lingers, a tender gaze.
Glows of warmth in the gentle dark,
Whispers held in a sacred spark.

Notes of silence, a serenade sweet,
Embracing all with a rhythmic beat.
The weave of dreams in the twilight show,
A harmony found in the ebb and flow.

Fluttering hearts in the velvet night,
Bathed in the glow, spirits take flight.
Each sound a caress, each moment a gift,
In the softness where souls uplift.

Together they dance, dreams intertwine,
Creating a world where all is divine.
A symphony held in the night's soft throe,
In the embrace of softness and glow.

Celestial Ballet of Light and Dark

In the canvas of night, stars arise,
Dancing gently in velvet skies.
Moonlight whispers on silent trees,
Awakening dreams wrapped in soft breeze.

Shadows stretch where the daylight fades,
In the heart of dusk, the world cascades.
Light and dark in a graceful waltz,
Every moment, a perfect impulse.

Constellations weave tales of lore,
Guiding sailors to distant shores.
As twilight deepens, colors blend,
The celestial ballet, without end.

An eternal spin, a cosmic dance,
In every heartbeat, a second chance.
Light and dark, forever tight,
In this celestial wonder of endless night.

Embrace of the Soft and the Brilliant

Morning whispers with tender rays,
Softly waking the world in praise.
Golden hues brush across the dew,
A gentle touch, a love so true.

Brilliant laughter from blooms in spring,
Nature's symphony begins to sing.
Petals glisten in bright display,
Softened hearts welcome the day.

As daylight lingers, shadows play,
In warm embraces, they find their way.
The soft and brilliant, hand in hand,
Crafting beauty, an endless strand.

In twilight's grace, colors unfold,
Stories of life in shades of gold.
Together they dance, a timeless song,
Where soft and brilliant forever belong.

The Sun's Caress on Silken Swells

Waves shimmer bright in the dawn's warm glow,
The sun's gentle touch in a radiant flow.
Kisses of light on the ocean's face,
Wrap the world in a warm embrace.

Sailboats drift on the silken sea,
Caught in the magic, wild and free.
Wash of tide, a soothing balm,
Lapping softly, the ocean's calm.

Golden splendor dances with grace,
Nature's canvas in endless space.
Touched by the sun, each swell and crest,
In this quiet moment, hearts find rest.

The horizon glows in fiery hues,
Promising joy in every muse.
With every wave that merges and swells,
The sun's caress, a tale it tells.

Mellow Breezes and Luminous Peaks

Mellow breezes sway the trees,
Whispers of nature, soft like keys.
Under the azure, the world unfolds,
Gentle adventures waiting, bold.

Luminous peaks kiss the gentle sky,
Inviting us to dream and fly.
With every shadow, a story gleams,
Mountains cradle our wildest dreams.

As twilight drapes its silken veil,
The hike begins on a winding trail.
Breezes carry scents of pine,
In every step, the heart aligns.

Atop the heights, where eagles soar,
Mellow whispers of the earth's core.
Where breezes blend with heights so steep,
In luminous moments, our souls leap.

Veil of Serendipity

In the mist of chance we find,
Fleeting moments intertwined.
Paths of grace and fate align,
In the heart, a spark divine.

Whispers dance on dusky air,
Secrets held beyond compare.
Every turn, a new surprise,
Glimmers caught in passing eyes.

Silent echoes softly speak,
In the search, the bold, the meek.
Magic brews in every glance,
Life reveals its hidden dance.

Embrace the twist of time's embrace,
In each moment's sweet trace.
Serendipity unfolds,
Stories waiting to be told.

A Canvas of Moments

Brushstrokes of laughter and tears,
Painting life through passing years.
Every shade a tale to share,
Captured dreams floating in air.

Colors blend in twilight's glow,
Silhouettes of love we know.
Memories crisp with the night,
Canvas woven with pure light.

In the gallery of the heart,
Each moment plays a vital part.
Captured time, unyielding grace,
Life's masterpiece we embrace.

Threads of joy and whispers blend,
On this canvas, dreams extend.
In every hue, a world we weave,
In this art, we dare believe.

Morning Drizzle and Golden Rays

Gentle drops from skies descend,
Nature's kiss, the day will send.
Whispers soft upon the grass,
Moments linger, time will pass.

Golden rays break through the grey,
Bathe the world in bright array.
Every droplet sparkles, glows,
In the light, a magic flows.

Freshness fills the waking air,
Hope and peace beyond compare.
Morning whispers, sweet and bright,
Guiding us to new delight.

In this dance of light and shade,
Dreams awaken, unafraid.
Morning drizzles gently play,
With golden rays throughout the day.

Whispers of Daylight and Shade

In the hush of dawn's soft light,
Shadows pause, retreating night.
Glimmers flicker, shadows sway,
Whispers weave through brightening day.

Softly sigh the sunlit beams,
Drifting through our waking dreams.
Nature breathes, a gentle balm,
In the quiet, found a calm.

Between the sun and shaded trees,
Where time flows slow like a breeze.
Each moment holds a secret song,
In the daylight, we belong.

Dancing between light and dark,
Life unfolds its hidden arc.
In these whispers, we shall find,
Both the light and dark entwined.

Portals of Laughter and Lingering Twilight

In the dimming light we find,
Whispers of joy that bind.
Laughter echoes through the space,
A dance of shadows, a warm embrace.

Beneath the twilight's fading glow,
Memories linger, soft and slow.
Every smile, a fleeting spark,
Lighting up the gentle dark.

With every step, we move in flow,
Portals open where spirits grow.
The night invites the stars to play,
In laughter's realm, we drift away.

In this moment, time suspends,
A tapestry where joy extends.
Lingering twilight leads the way,
Portals of laughter into the day.

The Wayward Journey of Light and Shadow

Wanderers of both light and dark,
Tracing paths with gentle spark.
The moon's soft gaze on quiet streams,
Illuminates our shifting dreams.

Through the forest, shadows creep,
Secrets buried, whispers deep.
Dancing beams through branches weave,
A tapestry of what we believe.

Light and shadow, hand in hand,
Together dance across the land.
Echoes echo, fading away,
In the silence, thoughts hold sway.

Journeys twist, horizons bend,
Every journey has no end.
With each heartbeat, we are found,
Light and shadow, forever bound.

Trails Marked by Their Silent Pass

Footprints linger on the ground,
Silent echoes, softly found.
The past speaks through the trees,
Whispered secrets in the breeze.

Each trail tells a story old,
Of dreams pursued and hearts bold.
In the rustle of the leaves,
Reside the hopes each spirit weaves.

Through the thickets, paths unwind,
Every step, a tale defined.
In the twilight, shadows blend,
As the day begins to end.

Mark the trails with quiet grace,
Embrace the journey, find your place.
In the silence, let it last,
Navigating through the past.

Breezes of Nostalgia under Luminous Skies

Under skies where lanterns gleam,
Breezes carry whispers, dreams.
Nostalgia weaves a tender thread,
For moments lived, for words unsaid.

Echoes of laughter fill the air,
As memories dance without a care.
Stars above like watchful eyes,
Guide our hearts with soft replies.

Every gust a gentle sigh,
Reminders of the days gone by.
The past and present intertwine,
In every breeze, a sacred sign.

Luminous skies, a canvas wide,
Where our memories often hide.
In the stillness, let them flow,
Breezes of nostalgia, forever aglow.

Whispers of the Skies

Gentle winds that softly sigh,
Carrying secrets from up high.
Clouds in a dance, swirling free,
Whispers of dreams call out to me.

Stars twinkle in the velvet night,
Guiding lost souls with their light.
Moonbeams drape a silver veil,
A tranquil peace, a sweet exhale.

Birds take flight at break of dawn,
Painting the sky as they yawn.
Colors blend in a vivid show,
Whispers of the skies softly flow.

As twilight falls, hues intertwine,
Nature's canvas, oh so divine.
In the quiet, I hear the call,
Whispers of the skies, enchanting all.

A Tapestry of Light and Shadow

Sunlight kisses the forest floor,
Nature's tapestry, forevermore.
Shadows dance beneath the trees,
A symphony sways with the breeze.

Golden rays in the morning glow,
Interlaced with a soft shadow.
Colors weave from bright to dark,
Painting life with a vibrant spark.

Evening falls with a gentle sigh,
Colors fade as the day waves goodbye.
In the dusk, stories have spun,
A tapestry woven, all is one.

Embracing light, embracing shade,
In every heart, a bond is made.
Together they dance, never apart,
A timeless work of collaborative art.

The Dance of Daydreams

In the quiet of a wandering mind,
Daydreams swirl, a world unconfined.
Colors burst in swirling hues,
Imagination sings, nothing to lose.

Floating softly on a gentle breeze,
Moments captured, hearts at ease.
Fantasies twirl in a waltz so sweet,
With every thought, I feel complete.

Casting shadows of hopes untold,
Weaving visions, gentle and bold.
In this dance, I lose my way,
Finding joy in dreams that sway.

As daylight fades, the night arrives,
In the stillness, my spirit thrives.
The dance of daydreams never ends,
Through every heartbeat, my soul transcends.

When Radiance Meets Gray

Morning breaks with a brilliant glare,
Golden rays meet the soft gray air.
A clash of colors, a sight so rare,
When radiance meets the depth of despair.

Clouds drift by in a fleeting embrace,
Sunshine peeks, illuminating space.
In the struggle, beauty unfolds,
A story written in hues of gold.

As day deepens, shadows grow long,
In the twilight, both weak and strong.
Harmony blooms in the turning skies,
When radiance meets gray, hope never dies.

At day's end, as colors blend,
With every sunset, our hearts transcend.
Whispers of promise in the night,
When radiance meets gray, all feels right.

The Mirage of Radiance

In deserts vast, where shadows play,
The sunbeams dance, then fade away.
A glimmer soft, yet hard to find,
It beckons forth, then leaves behind.

A shimmering veil, so thin and bright,
Whispers of gold in the fading light.
With every step, the vision sways,
A fleeting dream through sunlit rays.

Yet hope persists, amid the sand,
Chasing the glow, with outstretched hand.
Though visions fade, the heart will yearn,
For mirage dreams, the spirit burns.

In every gleam, a tale unfolds,
Of radiant quests, and legends told.
They mesmerize, but slip away,
Into the dusk of a dying day.

Hues of Hope

In skies adorned with colors bright,
The dawn breaks forth, a wondrous sight.
Each hue a promise, warm and bold,
Revealing dreams yet to unfold.

The oranges blend with shades of blue,
Creating worlds where wishes grew.
Beneath the arch of radiant skies,
We find the strength to rise and rise.

The canvas broad, where heartbeats sing,
In every stroke, the hope we bring.
Through storms we weather, colors blend,
A masterpiece, where hearts transcend.

As twilight falls, the colors fade,
Yet in our souls, their warmth is laid.
For hope retains its vibrant glow,
In every heart, the hues will flow.

Sunlit Secrets

Beneath the trees, where shadows dance,
The daylight weaves a fleeting glance.
In every ray, a secret lies,
A hidden truth that gently sighs.

The whispers soft, in golden beams,
Unravel tales of childhood dreams.
They speak of love in summer's breath,
Of life that flourishes, defying death.

Through laughter bright and quiet sighs,
The sunlit paths where friendship flies.
In moments shared, the magic grows,
In every heart, the sunlight glows.

As evenings fall, the secrets blend,
Into the night, where dreams ascend.
Yet in the dark, some light remains,
The sunlit secrets, love sustains.

Flickering Whispers

In twilight's gloom, where shadows play,
Flickering whispers guide the way.
A haunting tune from the distant past,
Echoes soft, yet fading fast.

Through rustling leaves, the stories creep,
Awakening dreams from slumber deep.
With every sigh, a moment shared,
The flickers spark, a heart laid bare.

Beneath the stars, where secrets swim,
In the hush of night, the lights grow dim.
Yet in this dark, the whispers call,
A flickering hope, uniting all.

Through shadows deep, we'll find our way,
With flickering whispers, night and day.
For in their glow, our spirits rise,
Transcending fears beneath the skies.

A Story Woven in Vapor and Radiance

In whispers soft, the dawn does speak,
A tale of dreams, both bright and meek.
Through misty paths where shadows dance,
We find the glow, a fleeting chance.

Each droplet caught, a world anew,
In shimmering light, all thoughts imbue.
With every breath, we weave a thread,
In vapor soft, where hearts are led.

The tapestry glows, both warm and cold,
Of moments lost and secrets told.
A journey spun from hope and fear,
In radiant hues, we draw them near.

As night retreats, and stars take flight,
Our story claims the tender night.
With every pulse, the night gives way,
To stories woven, come what may.

Glistening Paths through the Veil

In twilight hush, the paths unfold,
A shimmering tale that must be told.
Through veils of mist, the secrets gleam,
In glistening light, we chase the dream.

Each step we take, a spark ignites,
In silent woods, where magic lights.
The whispers call from shadows deep,
Awake the hopes that silence keep.

With every turn, the glimmers fade,
Yet in our hearts, their warmth is laid.
Through winding trails of silver sheen,
We find the world, so fresh, so green.

And as we walk, the dawn appears,
To wash away the lingering fears.
The paths we tread in glistening grace,
Lead us to time and sacred space.

Light's Promise in Gloomy Realms

In shadows deep, where silence dwells,
A flicker stirs, and softly swells.
With every breath, the light will grow,
In gloomy realms, the promise flows.

Each moment faced, we seek the spark,
To guide us through the endless dark.
A flickering flame, so warm, so bright,
In darkened woods, it brings delight.

With trembling hands, we grasp the glow,
In every heart, the fire can show.
Through trials faced, our spirits soar,
In light's embrace, we learn to roar.

So linger not in shadows' clutch,
For light will rise, that sacred touch.
In every dawn, a vow remains,
Light's promise bright, through all our pains.

Patterns of Serenity and Fire

In calming hues, the day unfolds,
With patterns bright, and stories bold.
In gentle grace, the world aligns,
With rhythms soft, as heart defines.

In flickering flame, our spirits dance,
In moments caught, we chance romance.
Through swirling trails of quiet sighs,
We touch the stars, we dare to rise.

Each heartbeat sings, a melody,
In patterns wild, we seek to be.
A tapestry of joy and pain,
In fire's glow, we break the chain.

So let the light weave through the night,
Embrace the warmth, and share the sight.
For in the blend of calm and blaze,
We find our truth in endless ways.

Embrace of the Ether

In the silence of the night,
Whispers dance on gossamer light,
Stars weave tales from afar,
Embraced beneath the cosmic star.

Breath of twilight fills the air,
Guiding hearts, tender and rare,
A harmony of dreams takes flight,
Cradled in the arms of night.

Waves of time gently flow,
Rustling secrets, soft and low,
In the space where thoughts entwine,
We find solace, pure and divine.

Infinite like a gentle stream,
We awaken to the dream,
In the ether, love's sweet grace,
The universe, our warm embrace.

Glistening Veils and Hidden Hues

Beneath the rainbow's soft embrace,
Whispers linger, finding grace,
Colors blend, a secret art,
Glistening veils, a tuneful heart.

Each shade tells a story bold,
Of dreams and wishes yet untold,
Hidden hues in shadows played,
In their depths, our hopes conveyed.

Draped in light, we spin and sway,
Painting moments, night and day,
A canvas rich with whispered tones,
Where laughter breathes, and love atones.

In the gallery of the soul,
Every shade makes us whole,
Glistening veils, a dance anew,
In every heart, a hidden hue.

Laughter through the Veil

Through the veil of time we peek,
Echoes of laughter, soft and sleek,
Moments captured, forever bright,
In the warmth of shared delight.

Glimmers of joy in twilight's glow,
Stories of old, in whispers flow,
Each giggle finds its way back home,
In the heart, no need to roam.

We weave our tales with playful sighs,
In a world painted with sunny skies,
Through the veil, we see so clear,
Laughter's song, a tune so dear.

In every heartbeat, in every call,
Connection blossoms, enriching all,
United through the laughter's grace,
A timeless dance, a warm embrace.

Sunkissed Dreams

Golden rays adorn the dawn,
Whispers warm, like a gentle yawn,
Sunkissed dreams take flight anew,
In the morn, all things feel true.

Fields of gold, where wishes lay,
Awakened hopes greet the day,
Sunlight dances on every stream,
A symphony of light, a dream.

With every step, the world aglow,
Nature sings, and spirits flow,
In the embrace of warmth and cheer,
Each moment cherished, held so dear.

As daylight fades to evening's call,
Sunkissed dreams linger for all,
In our hearts, they softly gleam,
Forever held, a precious dream.

9 789916 889114